Fight
On!

GLORIA COPELAND

Kenneth Copeland Publications
Fort Worth, Texas

Fight On!

ISBN 1-57562-054-5   30-0539

All scripture is from the *King James Version*
unless otherwise noted.

Kenneth Copeland Publications
Fort Worth, Texas 76192-0001

Fight On!

"I'm tired of fighting! As soon as I whip one problem, there are a hundred more knocking at my door!"

Some years ago a friend of mine said those very words to the Lord. At the time, she was weary from the battles of life and ministry. She was fatigued from the constant pressure of pushing back the powers of darkness in her own life and in the lives of those around her. I'll never forget the Lord's response to her as she voiced her frustration.

What is an army for, if not to fight? He said. *You'll either be fighting or retreating from now until Jesus returns!*

Those words come as a shock to many Christians. They don't want to be warriors. They want a comfortable, easy life. They want to lie back, take it easy and go on a spiritual vacation. But that's not what we as believers are called to do.

We're called to *"Fight the good fight of faith"* (1 Timothy 6:12). We are an army and we are at war, *"not against flesh and blood, but against principalities, against powers, against the rulers of the darkness of this world, against spiritual wickedness in high places"* (Ephesians 6:12).

God has given us spiritual weapons that are *"...mighty through God to the pulling down of strong holds"* (2 Corinthians 10:4). He has given us His own armor (see Ephesians 6:10-18). In other words, He has equipped us to be spiritual soldiers in the army of the Lord.

Victorious Words From a
Victorious Soldier

Now, in every army there are good soldiers and sloppy soldiers. There are soldiers who win battles and conquer enemy territory, and there are soldiers who fail and lose ground. I want to be a good soldier for the Lord, don't you? I want to drive the devil back and advance the kingdom of God.

The Apostle Paul was that kind of soldier. He was a man of victory. He triumphed in every circumstance. The devil tried to stop him again and again with persecutions, beatings and trouble of every kind. But Paul kept right on marching in victory, preaching the gospel, healing the sick, working miracles and building the Church of the Lord Jesus Christ.

Eventually, Paul was put in prison and in chains. Imagine how terrible the conditions in prison must have been in those days! No doubt, the devil expected that to stop Paul—but it didn't. Instead of lying down and feeling sorry for himself, Paul used his time in prison to write most of the New Testament. Prison didn't *even* slow him down.

Just look at the victorious words Paul wrote when his life on this earth was through:

The time of my departure is at hand. I have fought a good fight, I have finished my course, I have kept the faith: Henceforth there is laid up for me a crown of righteousness, which the Lord, the righteous judge, shall give me at that day: and not to me only, but unto all them also that love his appearing (2 Timothy 4:6-8).

Aren't those wonderful words? I want to be able to say words like that when I come to the end of my earthly life. I want to know that I have fought the good fight—and won!

Someone might say, "Well, Gloria, that was the Apostle Paul! He was special. We can't all be like him."

Why not? We have the same Savior Paul had. We're filled with the same Holy Spirit. We even have the words he wrote to Timothy, his precious son in the faith, just before he departed this life—instructions that Paul knew would enable Timothy to be a victorious soldier of the Cross just as he had been.

Endure Hardness

What were those instructions? You can find one of them in 2 Timothy 2:3.

There Paul says, *"Thou therefore endure hardness, as a good soldier of Jesus Christ."*

Notice Paul didn't say, *"If* hard times come, endure them." He simply said, "Endure hardness."

There are no "ifs" about it. Hard times are going to come in the life of every believer. There will be times when circumstances will seem dark, times when you face seemingly impossible obstacles, times when defeat seems inevitable.

Some Christians get confused when those times come. "What's happening here?" they cry. "I thought Jesus redeemed me from the curse!"

He did, but you can rest assured, Satan will challenge that redemption. He will try his best to steal it from you by pulling you off your walk of faith. Jesus warned us about that in the parable of the sower. He said:

> **The sower soweth the word. And these are they by the way side, where the word is sown; but when they have heard, Satan cometh immediately, and taketh away the word that was sown in their hearts. And these are they likewise which are sown on stony ground; who, when they have heard the word, immediately receive it with gladness; And have no root in themselves, and so endure but for a time: afterward, when affliction or persecution ariseth for the word's sake, immediately they are offended (Mark 4:14-17).**

Satan will not sit idly by while you sail through life, effortlessly believing the Word of God. He'll pressure you with hard times. He'll attack you with sickness or lack, then he'll lie to you and tell you that God doesn't care. He'll try to convince you that God is not going to answer your prayer this time. He'll attempt to talk you into believing there's no way out and you're going to end up a miserable failure.

When those hard times come, don't cave in to the pressure. Don't give up. Stand on the Word of God and endure hardness like a good soldier.

Soldiers will put up with far more discomfort than civilians. Have you ever noticed that? A soldier in boot camp will jump out of bed before dawn every morning to run and do push-ups. He may not like it, but he'll do it because his commanding officer has ordered him to do it. He endures the discomfort because he knows it's an inescapable part of military life.

A civilian, on the other hand, might start an exercise program but when the going gets tough, his muscles feel sore and his schedule gets busy, he'll just quit exercising. If someone asks him about it, he might just shrug and say, "I tried exercise, but it didn't work for me."

Some Christians are like that. They hear the Word of faith and they think, *Well, I'll try that.* Then when the hard times come, they give up.

But that's not how it should be. After all, we're not civilians! We're soldiers! We don't *try* faith, we make it our lifestyle. We walk by faith whether it's hard or easy. We don't do it so we'll be blessed. We do it because we're determined to be pleasing to Jesus. He is our commander in chief, and the Bible says *"without faith it is impossible to please him!"* (Hebrews 11:6).

Of course, we *will* end up blessed if we'll walk by faith. We'll end up healed and delivered and prospering in every area of life because God promised we would. That, however, is not our motivation. We're motivated by our desire to serve the Lord. That's what makes us believe His Word, stand fast and endure when the hard times come.

Beware of Trivial Pursuits

As soldiers, we must also realize it's not just the hard times that are dangerous. It's the good times too. Sometimes the pleasures and seemingly harmless distractions of this world can draw us away from the plans and purposes of God just as surely as persecutions and afflictions. They can hinder us in the day of battle. That's why Paul said, *"No soldier when in service gets entangled*

*in the enterprises of [civilian] life; his
aim is to satisfy and please the one
who enlisted him"* (2 Timothy 2:4,
The Amplified Bible).

In the years I've lived by faith, I've
noticed that it's easy to get entangled
in the affairs of this life. In fact, it
sometimes seems like this world is
like an octopus always trying to grab
you with its tentacles. If you don't
watch out, it will wrap itself around
you until you're completely caught
up in the mundane, trivial things of
this world.

If you let them, those trivial pur-
suits will hold you down and keep
you from soaring on into the eternal
things of God. They will choke out
the Word that has been planted in
your heart and leave you without
faith and without power.

Jesus said it like this:

The ones sown among the thorns are others who hear the Word, Then the cares and anxieties of the world, and distractions of the age, and the pleasure and delight and false glamour and deceitfulness of riches, and the craving and passionate desire for other things creep in and choke and suffocate the Word, and it becomes fruitless (Mark 4:18-19, _The Amplified Bible_).

Here in the United States, we must be especially vigilant against such entanglements because we have such an abundance of material possessions! We can easily end up spending all our time just taking care of them all.

As the Lord told a friend of mine in prayer one day, this nation has become a nation of maintenance men.

We maintain our house. We maintain our yard. We maintain our car and our hair, our nails and our clothes. The problem is, by the time we've done what it takes to maintain all the natural things in our lives, we often don't have any time left to maintain the spirit man who lives on the inside of us.

Has that happened to you? If so, as a good soldier, there's only one thing for you to do: *simplify your life.*

"But Gloria," you say, "the things I do are important. I can't just cut them out of my life!"

Listen, there's nothing more important than spending time with God in prayer and in the Word. The time you spend with Him will not only enable you to succeed in this life, but it will help you build for eternity. It will bear fruit that lasts forever.

So make whatever adjustments you must make to spend time with God. Refuse to let anything rob you of it. Whenever you take on anything new, count the cost—not just in money, but in time. Ask yourself, *Can I afford this spiritually? Can I spare the precious hours and minutes this project (possession, hobby, etc.) will require and still have plenty of time to fellowship with the Lord?*

If the answer is *no*, then set that project aside.

I realize that may mean passing up some things you enjoy. But remember, as a good soldier, your aim is not to please yourself. It's to please the One Who enlisted you. And believe me, when you make sacrifices for Him, He always makes sure you're well rewarded—not only in this age, but in the age to come.

Look Up!

Right now you may be thinking, *My, this soldier business sounds rough. I'm not sure if I can do it.*

Yes, you can!

How? By following two more golden words of advice the Apostle Paul gave Timothy:

1. *"Constantly keep in mind Jesus Christ, the Messiah, [as] risen from the dead..."* (2 Timothy 2:8, *The Amplified Bible*).

2. *"Continue to hold to the things that you have learned..."* (2 Timothy 3:14, *The Amplified Bible*).

When you face the pressure of battle, when stress and trouble come, when you feel you're about to faint, look up! Focus your attention on the heavenly truth that Jesus Christ has risen from the dead and you are in Him! That means when He arose, you arose. When He defeated the devil, you defeated the devil. His victory is your victory!

Think about that when the devil is telling you that you're not going to make it. Then turn the tables on him and tell *him* a few things for a change! Say:

Satan, I remind you that Jesus triumphed over you. I remind you that He spoiled you and made a show of you; that He took away all the authority you had. The Bible says you've been brought to naught! You're nothing, but I am Jesus' own representative here on the earth. I have His power and act in His Name. I'm seated with Him in heavenly places. All I have to do is stand in the victory Jesus has already won. The only way

you can defeat me is by convinc-
ing me to quit and that's the one
thing I won't do! I won't accept
defeat. I won't let you talk me out
of my victory. I will stand and
endure until I win—so you might
as well surrender right now.

Or, just say:

"In the Name of Jesus, get out of my presence!"

That's the way a good soldier talks. And that's the way you'll talk too when you constantly keep in mind Christ Jesus has risen from the dead! That's the way you'll think when you turn your attention away from the impossible problems before you and focus instead on God with Whom all things are possible. As Colossians 3:1-4 says:

If then you have been raised to life with Christ, your heart must be set on the great

realities of that heavenly sphere, where Christ is seated at the right hand of God. Your constant concern must be with the heavenly realities, not with worldly trivialities. For you died to this world, and now you have entered with Christ into the secret life of God. When Christ, who is your life, comes again for all the world to see, then all the world will see that you too share his glory *(A New Translation by William Barclay)*.

Keep Marching

Once you've set your mind on things above and you've begun to talk the victory, simply continue to do the things you've learned. In other words, keep marching!

Keep reading and meditating on the Word. Keep acting in faith. That's really all it takes to win even the most complicated battles.

You don't have to know all the answers to your situation. You don't need a great amount of talent or ability. God has all the ability you could ever need and He knows all the answers, so all you have to do is trust Him and continue doing what you know to do.

Notice, I said continue *doing*. Just thinking about it won't work. Just knowing it won't get you through. It is not what you know that counts in this fight of faith—it is what you do!

James 2:26 says that faith without corresponding action is dead. So take action! Don't just say you believe God's Word, act like you believe it.

If you will do that, you'll suffer no defeat. You might experience a few temporary setbacks, but you will triumph in the end. And when your life in this earth is through, you'll be able to say those glorious words once written by the Apostle Paul: *"I have fought a good fight, I have finished my course, I have kept the faith!"* (2 Timothy 4:7). You'll be able to stand tall for eternity as a victorious soldier of the Lord. And Jesus will be able to say to you, "Well done, good and faithful servant!"

Prayer for Salvation
and Baptism in the Holy Spirit

Heavenly Father, I come to You in the Name of Jesus. Your Word says, *"...whosoever shall call on the name of the Lord shall be saved"* (Acts 2:21). I am calling on You. I pray and ask Jesus to come into my heart and be Lord over my life according to Romans 10:9-10. *"If thou shalt confess with thy mouth the Lord Jesus, and shalt believe in thine heart that God hath raised him from the dead, thou shalt be saved."* I do that now. I confess that Jesus is Lord, and I believe in my heart that God raised Him from the dead.

I am now reborn! I am a Christian—a child of Almighty God! I am saved! You also said in Your Word, *"If ye then, being evil, know how to give good gifts unto your children: HOW MUCH MORE shall your heavenly Father give the Holy Spirit to them that ask him?"* (Luke 11:13). I'm also asking You to fill me with the Holy Spirit. Holy Spirit, rise up within me as I praise God. I fully expect to speak with other tongues as You give me the utterance (Acts 2:4).

Begin to praise God for filling you with the Holy Spirit. Speak those words and syllables you receive—not in your own language, but the language given to you by the Holy Spirit. You have to use your own voice. God will not force you to speak.

Now you are a Spirit-filled believer. Continue with the blessing God has given you and pray in tongues each day. You'll never be the same!

Find a good Word of God preaching church, and become a part of a church family who will love and care for you as you love and care for them.

We need to be hooked up to each other. It increases our strength in God. It's God's plan for us.

Books by Kenneth Copeland

*Available in Spanish

Books by Gloria Copeland

* And Jesus Healed Them All
  Are You Ready?
  Build Yourself an Ark
  From Faith to Faith—A Daily Guide to Victory
  God's Prescription for Divine Health
  God's Success Formula
* God's Will for You
  God's Will for Your Healing
  God's Will Is Prosperity
  God's Will Is the Holy Spirit
* Harvest of Health
  Healing Promises
  Love—The Secret to Your Success
  No Deposit—No Return
  Pressing In—It's Worth It All
  The Power to Live a New Life
  The Unbeatable Spirit of Faith
* Walk in the Spirit
  Walk With God
  Well Worth the Wait

*Available in Spanish

Other Books Published by KCP

Heirs Together by Mac Hammond
John G. Lake—His Life, His Sermons,
    His Boldness of Faith
Winning the World by Mac Hammond

World Offices
of Kenneth Copeland Ministries

For more information about KCM and a free catalog, please write the office nearest you:

Kenneth Copeland Ministries
Fort Worth, Texas 76192-0001

Kenneth Copeland
Locked Bag 2600
Mansfield Delivery Centre
QUEENSLAND 4122
AUSTRALIA

Kenneth Copeland
Post Office Box 15
BATH
BA1 1GD
ENGLAND

Kenneth Copeland
Post Office Box 830
RANDBURG
2125
REPUBLIC OF SOUTH AFRICA

Kenneth Copeland
Post Office Box 58248
Vancouver
BRITISH COLUMBIA
V6P 6K1
CANADA

220123 MINSK
REPUBLIC OF BELARUS
Post Office 123
P/B 35
Kenneth Copeland Ministries